T0153218

Absolutely

M A Y B E

Nick Anthony Russo

NICK ANTHONY RUSSO

Absolutely Maybe
©2019 by NICK ANTHONY RUSSO

Published by Clover Croft Publishing, Franklin, Tennessee
Published in association with Larry Carpenter of Clover Croft, LLC
www.christianbookservices.com
Photo credit for cover art by Gil Bruvel
Cover Design by Suzanne Lawing and Tiarra Tompkins
Interior Layout Design by Debbie Manning Sheppard
Edited by Adept Content Solutions.
978-1-948484-45-9
Printed in the United States of America

Dedicated

To Mom,
With Love

Acknowledgments

I want to thank Tiarra Tompkins
and the team at OnFire Books.
Their hard work and dedication has
made it possible for me to see
my vision realized.

I also want to thank Larry Carpenter
at Clovercroft publishing
for believing in my book and mission.
Debbie Manning Sheppard for creating
a layout design that truly spoke to
each piece of poetry and prose,
to Suzanne Lawing for her help taking
my cover concept and making it a reality and finally
to Gil Bruvel for giving me the chance to use
your incredible artwork for the cover.
Without each of you, this book would not be here,
inspiring people to take that deeper journey with words.
Truly, I cannot thank each of you enough
for your patience and support.

If someone you are in a
relationship with
is not kind and not generous
to your spirit,
you must let them GO—
you are but a
ghost
to them, anyhow.
For them, you will always be
invisible
to what they put first,
as they only see
through you and beyond you
for whatever else it is they seek.
They are not truly contented
with you by their side, and,
upon such hard self-realization,
none may discredit you,
for like a moth to flame
we are sometimes drawn
to what is most bad for us.
But, when the scales do finally tip,
to which they always do, and
FAVOR grants you
HER calming clarity
and you are able to
BREAK THE CHAINS THAT BIND,
it may very well be
YOU
that haunts them
by mere absence alone.

You must do something.
SOMETHING DIFFERENT.

You don't fear failure.
WHAT YOU FEAR IS SUCCESS.

This world is not too big for you.
YOU ARE TOO **BIG** FOR THIS WORLD. AND THAT
YOU ARE TOO **BIG** FOR THIS WORLD,

why pretend and play small?

If you continue to expect failure,
YOU SHALL HAVE IT.

This way of thinking
CAN **ONLY RESULT IN A SELF-PROPHECY** OF DOOM.

Granted, I am aware
THAT THERE IS A CERTAIN COMFORT **IN YOUR DEFEAT**
BECAUSE YOU THINK IT PRESERVES YOU,

and self-preservation
IS THE MOST NATURAL OF INSTINCTS.

That is why you must

change your own trajectory
BY CHANGING YOUR ATTITUDE POSITIVELY
TOWARD YOURSELF
AND, BY INFERENCE,
THE WORLD THAT SURROUNDS YOU.

Expect success
BY MANIFESTING
WHAT YOU FEAR MOST,
your own success.

If he doesn't love you, I will.
If he chooses to leave you, I'll stay.
If he goes on without you, I never will.

—God

Can you love me
in the in-between moments of our euphoria?

If you can and if you do,
then you do—no question.

I don't need to be happy.
I need to have

faith.

**I have wasted a lot of precious time
feeling shameful for my past.**
But, once I learned how to
truly forgive myself,
I could instantly recognize people around
me for who themselves had yet not.
It is a very wise thing to be kind to yourself,
but it wiser still to be kinder
to those that are still trying to
reconcile with themselves
what you have managed to achieve.
Be keenly aware the difference,
and humbly teach what
you have been lovingly taught.

I grew into my power.

Not because I wanted to,

but rather,

because

*I **HAD** to.*

We are not fools.

We each know very well the difference

between who kisses us with their lips

and who kisses us with their heart.

We need to be equal

in all things between us.

Pulling the weight.

Pushing the stars.

You have not seen
my fire
until you have felt it.

As I burn,

you burn.

We are all things

together,

the very bad, the very good.

True love is

E X P O S U R E .

True love is never certainty.

It is all risk or it is nothing.

Therein lies the beauty.

I tire of touching things that don't have meaning to me. My next embrace, I am certain, will reach so thoroughly and completely through another person that their ancestors will feel my steely breath upon the napes of their necks. My hands will touch too, and there **I will rewrite a new history down their spines, and I will traverse their memories with my fingers so far back and beyond to an epoch ancient where language wasn't yet even a mortal tool, just an indistinguishable utterance upon the tongues of those where only fire and a successful hunt mattered did sustain.** And when night does eventually return to its pitchest black, I'll lie on my back and there, looking straight up, I will hunt and gather the distant stars above me and make a gift to the future generations that will someday too walk Mother Earth.

I don't want to

worry

about you.

I want to worry

with

you.

The strongest

connection

between two people
is always in the
finding of one's self.

Strip me bare to the bone

because I can only **be** the person

that I **can be.**

Otherwise,

set me free at your own peril.

One day, your

cruelty

towards me
will exceed the many reasons I have
for still loving you.

No power on Earth

can make a woman

do what she doesn't want to do.

But when she so chooses to,

just sit back and get out of the way.

The only chance I took

that I ever regretted

was the only chance

I was never given

the chance
to ever take.

I like you much more

than any other

one thing

I think about you.

The road to perdition was paved

with the morsels of her desire.

Though her body hungered not any longer,

her spirit still craved the feast of forgiveness.

The most gratifying feeling
is the being next to someone
and not having the wanting of
anyone else.

Every man who wages war

believes God

is on his side.

I warrant God

should often wonder

who is on His.-

I am fire and I am fury.

My emotions stoked

by promises of my own making.

Catch up to me

or release me to

cinder.

Love doesn't adhere to a schedule,
so it never may be measured by time
any more than it would ever wait
to indulge your convenience.

I think about you all day.
There is just something about
you.
Can't place it.
DON'T WANT TO.

IF

you should ever lose yourself,

don't ever expect

someone else

to find your way back.

I see in you a
beauty
that others cannot see.
And if they think they do,
that is only what they think.
As for me, I know.
And that will always be
more than enough for me.

You never loved me
in a good way
love is loved.
You only loved me
in the way I helped you
hate yourself less.

There aren't any
COINCIDENCES;
there are only
CIRCUMSTANCES.

I don't have to be *first.*

I just have
to be equal

to the things *you love most.*

He wasn't perfect.

But he was just perfect enough

to show me that neither was I.

And in this, we each found quiet comfort.

He invaded her body like a

rampaging army.

His desire lay siege to her heart,

and there it encamped itself

for the unspoken conflict

that would resume between them.

Being

with someone

about their past

prior to knowing them

is equivalent to

being

about their future

before it happens.

A feeling like love is best when it

easily and naturally,
like moss over a stone.

You can't
make magic.
Magic
just happens...

I want to be wanted by you.

If I am not,

I will begin to drift.

And should I drift,

will be the only thing

left of me for you.

IF YOU WERE TO

DIG DEEPLY
ENOUGH

INTO SOMEBODY'S PAST,

YOU CAN BE ASSURED

THAT WHAT YOU'LL FIND

IS THAT YOU

AREN'T

PERFECT,
EITHER.

I did not know I had a heart.

You filled it with unknown creatures

whose names were

JOY and HOPE,

both sharper blades

than any had cut me before.

When you have

pressed your flesh to another's

beyond their ability to stay loyal,

it's easy to feel like a waste of skin.

COMPROMISE

is having the ability

of being able to

get your way

half of the time

all of the time.

New love

doesn't come to us quiet and slow.

It comes to us

raging like a

HURRICANE

and in its swathe of beauty,

old love is swept away.

During life

we comfort those who wish to die.

Nearing death

we comfort those who wish to live.

Flattery

WILL GET YOU EVERYWHERE,

BUT SO WILL ÜBER—

AND IT'S PROBABLY CHEAPER.

I really want to

WAKE

UP

next to someone

I REALLY WANT.

No more online

dating for me.

I finally

met someone

organically.

She is a plant.

Sometimes we can't

get what we need

any more than we can't

need what we get.

I think we are not here

to worry about ourselves.

I think we are here for a

GREATER
PURPOSE,

and that is to

SERVE
OTHERS.

may not have

much,

but

WE

have

much

of each other.

I will not quarrel with you

because I see your life a quarrel with itself.

When the world has turned,

find your true nature.

No one ever stopped her

dead in her tracks.

But the footprint

he left upon her heart

made forgetting

the best part of

remembering.

He lied to me.

I am gone from him

because I don't see his eyes any longer,

just the outline of his body,

and that was **never** enough.

God, she was as beautiful

as she was

unexpected.

It seemed like I had

waited all my life

for something I had

no idea I was missing.

I have been called a

hopeless romantic,

but in my mind

romance is never hopeless.

Just sometimes

the people involved in it are.

She was perfume to me.

I unstopped her when I needed to breathe her in,

and I sprayed her onto my body

when I had to be away from her.

WRITING
is sexy.
READING
is sexier.
COMPREHENDING
is sexiest.

Never give up

on your passion.

You never know

when it can inspire

someone else's.

She enjoyed dancing with the devil

but the only problem

was that she never really knew

when the music had

stopped.

No woman's beauty

had been more highly praised,

in every key

and in every instrument.

No heart

she ever stole

recovered it.

Oh yes,
they danced as only lovers could.
RHYTHM-LIKE CAGED FURIES
BETWEEN THEM,
tempered only by
WISDOM
and by a haste vetted.

WISDOM
*is when your
ugly heart
wants to speak,
but your
beautiful heart
won't let it.*

She loved herself

more than any disloyal lover ever could.

Her "ex" never marked her spot

because she never entrusted to him her map.

Today, I decided I no longer wanted to be your spoon.
I decided that you will no longer use me to cook you, to liquefy you,
and there to further take advantage of me by injecting the best parts of
myself inside of you so that I can remain your most illicit and devoted
enabler and drug. There is absolutely nothing recreational about me with
you! In fact, loving you, needing you, craving you, and being addicted
to you was the most lonely and ill-got of all my serious enterprises.
Therefore, you must understand, being a love junky was never my idea
of getting high, one where I was made to feel a vagabond on the streets,
destitute of both dignity and self-worth. I absent-mindedly found myself
standing upon the lonely corner of your heart, like some wide-eyed
beggar for change where you did deliberately avoid making eye contact
with me so you wouldn't be compelled to give me anything of real value
from your zipped-up tight phantom wallet that you called love.

But that was then and this is now. I am well aware of my folly and,
fortunately, I became to be arrested from the need of you only by the
grace of God. With His help, I am no longer your spoon. And that I am no
longer your spoon, I have unwittingly sobered you up in the process. You
don't ever even have to thank me. You see, I don't need the validation any
more than I need to make some sort of forced confession to a group of
seated strangers in a circle made up of expert story-tellers and human-
users like yourself. Instead, if you'd really care to be of assistance, I
would ask of you to be keenly aware that I was always much more than
just your paraphernalia, and I ha   ve, as of this moment, readily ceased
and desisted to further supply your hungered-up ego. And now that I
am in a much better place, I can only imagine your weighty withdrawals.
And now that I am in a much better place, I can only imagine you know
better what my own dependency was like. And now that I am in
a much better place, I can only welcome you to my
world, the one I've left far behind.

Nobody EVER promised you being beautiful was going to be EASY.

Yes, things happened fast between us. But that's how new love is.

It comes down upon us, torrential, unyielding, implacable. It can be no other way because if it were another way, it would not be nearly as wonderful or as frightfully painful. You see, what we have here between us is the makings of a true and lasting love—both the seed and the foundation. These are the necessary elements that, when distilled down to their most basic form, **one can't help but to become totally naked and transparent toward one another.** Invisible to others to be sure because we want for them not, but naked to one another because total exposure is the most remarkable way in which we come to love and, the most remarkable way in which we come to be loved. And that is precisely the beauty of us here upon this bookstore floor, where we did each share our deepest grief and, then, did too become more deeply bound by the joining of the most cerebral of ecstasies, as our bodies collided separately, then together reigned as one, because both our beautiful hearts held court over our lesser, but no less worthy, emotions. I now bow humbly before you, as you unknowingly brought me out from within my deepest slumber, as both love and pain are ought to do. And, then, from out of nowhere, you just laughed! You just plain laughed out loud!

But I didn't mind that—I didn't mind that at all—because I knew in that moment that that was your way in masking your own unimaginable things, just in the same way I masked my own. And finally, when your laugh did begin to slowly recede and completely slip away, I knew that, on this night, our bodies would not be made into one. I felt you had no idea of this, but I clearly did. You must understand that, ultimately, you did not belong to me, and in my mind, and in such perfect unison, I could not ever make that type of shift as you were never, and shall never, be but a mere possession to me. I took quiet comfort in this realization, and it becalmed me as we continued to sit, reigning together longer still for what appeared the briefest of eternities and I kept it that a way as long as I possibly could, because I just couldn't help myself from it because, **indeed, you are the rarest of treasures: your smile, your crown; your laugh, your scepter.** Having known you, no matter how briefly our time together was, I am a far better man for it. But this, like all temporal things, must sadly come to its inevitable conclusion. I know this true, even if you still do not. I want but to sleep, and I want but to forget. But I can't sleep so, instead, I compose here such deft melody, with love my fingers and with pain my keys, where piano did both

we orchestrate such sweet,
but not lasting, a harmony.

I miss the hell out of you
because I remember
the heaven within you.

She had been lied to so often that
all men's words seemed but harm.

Today, however,

she took in a new scent,
and it tasted safe.

We understand

more of what is hard

when we understand

more of what is impossible.

One day
I'll give you
the username and password
to my lips.
From there
you can take my tongue,
and we can
wipe your hard drive clean.

Even the patient,
mighty oak owes its

MAJESTIC LIFE

to the FRAGILE *and*

UNASSUMING ACORN.

You are

the one constant in my life.

Without you,

I am not me.

Imagination

is only the vessel.

Words

are the liquids

that fill it to the top.

Sometimes it is not about

you

not loving them enough;

sometimes it's just about

them

not loving themselves enough.

She often dreamt of

the one that got away.

But, she more happily awoke each morning

next to

the one

who never left her side.

A tempest raged inside her,

mixing a cocktail of her emotions

that poured out of her and into any man

that sobered and stilled her.

I like a slow **burn.**

There is something temporary

about a meteor that quick sizzles then fades.

I prefer an inextinguishable star.

Sexy, to me, has always been

a slow, hot burn.

She was both a
work of fiction and nonfiction.
I told her I wanted to start
from the back,
then work my way
slowly forward.

STRONG MEN *don't hurt you.* Weak men do.

I am thinking about you

constantly.

We haven't met yet,

but when we do,

 I'll know

immediately

that it was you

I was wanting all along.

What is a
CRUSH
but a tiger in a cage,
yet unreleased.

In a world of

instant gratification,

SHE TOOK MORE TIME

to truly know herself

than she did

trying to forget herself.

The
deepest
of our intimacies

is never the

cojoining of the hips.

They are only of

eye to eye,
of
hand to hand
and of
lip to lip..

Their love betrayed all sin
and made even loss feel
claustrophobic.
To say they loved one another deeply
was a lie falsely told.

It's okay to let him know. But once he does,
then it's his turn to reciprocate or not.
If he truly wants you, HE'LL SHOW YOU.

Of course, I could feel all of her weight
when she pressed down upon me.
She was thick with thought,
and she was heavy with emotion.

The thing we hate the most in people is very usually
the thing we hate the most about ourselves.

Faith
*is believing in something
just one more time beyond what you thought
yourself initially capable of.*

I get it.
You are
scared.

You don't want me to get too excited about you

because you don't want you to get

too excited about me.

The more

CONCESSIONS

we make about our character

for another person,

THE MORE WE BECOME
THE THINGS WE HATE

most within ourselves.

LITTLE THINGS

always constitute

the content of larger things.

That's why

THE DETAILS

matter in love.

If you truly

want to know the

composition of one's character,

watch how they behave

right after they don't get what they want.

Your journey

IS ETCHED IN YOUR SKIN

either by scar or ink.

Each drew blood.

Each tells a story.

Each is a reminder.

Expression heals.

What made her a woman to be reckoned with

wasn't just her curves,

but it was in her ability

to set you damn straight

if need be.

I like the way

you like me.

But I'd love the way

you'd love me

even better.

Even the

greatest of mysteries

can fade from us

if we don't water and feed them

just enough for them

to remain faithful to us.

As soon as you learn to dance
with a man,

THEN

you can love him.

My body

made love to her mind,

while my mind

made love to her body.

Are you hurt and damaged beyond repair?

Don't pity yourself—

just ask yourself how many men

have been on the dirty side of your storm.

Never

underestimate

a person's potential

in using personal details

you've shared with them about you

against you.

There was a time

in which I could not conceive

of how I ever was to forgive you.

Now, in this moment,

I am you.

She was a woman

beyond her time.

When the world

thought to silence

or disavow her,

SHE LOVED

LOUDER

and let go

EVEN TIGHTER.

In love again?

I always shall be
unless I can find
a better reason not to be.

The tears that roll the

s l o w e s t

down our face

are usually the ones

that have held in the

most
pain and
suffering.

I thought
he ruined,
brick by brick,
my ability to love.
I wish I knew then
that I wasn't crumbling
but just building up my foundation.

HAVING FUN

makes you forget.

BEING HAPPY

makes you remember.

FEELING CONTENT

makes you do both at the same time

BY BEING PRESENT.

It's very easy
to stop choosing
the same type of
wrong person
when you begin to
demand a lot more
of the right kind
of you.

Sadly,

the artistry of romance

has all but died

and has been replaced

by ineffectual texts

and the sound of a voice

no longer desired.

You hoard your pain
because the more you suffer,
the more the world becomes an

outrage.

You weep
because weeping
has become

evidence.

CHEMISTRY

is the trust between two people
rooted in comfort,
grown by commitment,
and then
bloomed
into an existence
most inexplicable.

It takes
balance
between two people
to stay together.
To push,
to pull
and there to govern the
strongest impulse
and not shut down.

When you love someone,

you worry for them.

When you haven't anyone to love,

you worry

you'll never love

or be loved again.

Perhaps,

God lives in the **non-believer**

as much as

He does in the **believer.**

When each our time comes,

what will separate us

may very well be

the heart

and not

just the belief.

We only truly discover how

FRAGILE

we are

when we are

made to realize how

STRONG

we've had to become.

The most gorgeous

of God's creations

are often the most fragile.

Never confuse beauty

with invulnerability.

I want to take a vacation

inside your body.

I want to work so hard

at loving you.

Beauty WITHOUT *charm*

IS JUST VANITY.

Our minds

are like

a chest of drawers,

wherein the dark recesses

lie the darkest memories.

Remind yourself

to empty them,

and often.

Humility

is the self-realization

upon the MOUNTAIN TOP

that all the people below you

appear just as small to you

as you do to them.

If you were free,

I'd **ravage** you.

But that you are not,

I ravage my imagination,

which is lesser,

BUT smarter.

Move on
to somebody

who can't stand

not seeing you.

We grow the most

when we suffer;

we live the most

when we love.

A N T I C I P A T I O N

made her wet,

BUT FEELING **SAFE**

made her wetter still.

Doesn't
matter
where.
Only matters
who.

I held her lips ransom
just as she held my tongue hostage,
and during that taut

exchange,

we negotiated by our hearts
and not by our minds.

When you aren't in love,

you have much more time

to reflect on what being in love

really means.

WOMEN

have gotten so far away

from being women because

MEN

have gotten so far away

from being men.

You paint me
BLACK.
And in that darkness,
you have forgotten
all of my many
wonderful
COLORS.

When we are able to

Openly talk

about

it,

we are likely getting better

about

it.

I sometimes feel
entirely defeated
by life's extremities.
Then I am reminded
of the smallest miracle
that is the
birth of a child.

The *last* thing I
needed
was the *first* thing
I wanted.

If you should ever feel

HATE

in your heart,

let it only be your rudder

but never your anchor.

Love
is so messy.
Hate
is so clean.

Have you ever not known
where you were going
*only to wind up
exactly where you
needed to be?*

Prayer without action

will never be a blessing

unless we learn

that neither are mutually exclusive

of one another.

Don't be so full of pride

that pride is all you have left.

Strip me bare to the bone

because I can only be

the person I can be.

Otherwise,

set me free

at your own peril.

I am looking for that
one
woman
I think of as
out of my league
just as she thinks
I am out of hers.

Fall in love
with someone who
tells you
that you are beautiful.
Fall more in love
with someone
who means it.

She knew she was a
disaster

waiting to happen.

But she also knew
her rescue crew
was
her own
abilities
and
her own
determination.

If I should
F
A
L
L
FAST,
just know that
I LOVE
HARD.

I am going to
so tear
you up!
But then,
I am going to
so put you
back
together
again.

Her name was
Truth.
She was
all the things
people thought
but were
too afraid to say.

I AM A
GHOST
NOT EVEN CAPABLE OF
HAUNTING
MY OWN BODY.

Oh,
I love you,
no doubt,
but don't you
dare think
for one second
that I have
stopped
having a
crush upon you.

HAPPINESS

is having enough.

CONTENTMENT

is realizing that you don't have enough,

but you are happy anyway.

When you are deeply in love,
the world does indeed
conform to your own blissful imaginings
and then,

magically,

transmutes itself yet again,
into an unfolding of

i n f i n i t e

possibilities.

I could love you to pieces
but I'd rather
      love you to whole.

I am so over you.
So here I hover uncontested,
your aching body
pulling me down
upon your own.
I am so over you.

We truly understand

FOR THE FIRST TIME

when we place our hands

upon whom we love.

You know,
if you weren't
part of this
relationship,
we'd be perfect

together.

When we are
FORCED TO STOP
loving a person,
we must always
RELEARN HOW
to love ourselves,
again.

MUCH OF WHAT WE CALL

PROGRESS

IS SIMPLY BEEN A MATTER OF

REMEMBERING
WHAT WAS ONCE
FORGOTTEN.

The more inured we become to being

A L O N E,

the harder it becomes for us to allow

SOMEONE

to be nearer us.

Intimacy

is the real

magic.

The woman sawed in half

IS JUST SEX.

I've committed
suicide
inside my head
so many times
that I've learned
to be thankful
my gun
was inside there too.

You know what I find

beautiful?

A woman
freshly awakened,
drinking a cup of coffee without a
stitch of
makeup on.

I have no idea
what I am looking for
until I find it.

It's always

changing

in who we are supposed to love

and who we are **not**.

The only thing

that stays the same

is that **we want**
who we want.

YOU

MUST

love a heart

like your own.

That is the only way

for love to

endure.

The rewards of
privilege
must always be tempered
with the
responsibilities
of CHARITY.

YOU CAN SOMETIMES BETTER

JUDGE

A MAN'S VALUES AND INTEGRITY

MORE BY WHAT HE DOES

AFTER HIS MARRIAGE THAN

DURING HIS MARRIAGE.

IT'S NOT

ALWAYS POSSIBLE

TO GET

THE ANSWERS WE NEED.

SOMETIMES

A PERSON'S ACTIONS

HAVE TO BE ENOUGH

FOR US JUST TO MOVE ON.

It so easy to become

victimized

by our own tragic story

that **we** often forget

that we are the

strongest
part

of the narrative.

He will only

APPEAR

to care

m**ore**

as soon as you begin to

APPEAR

to care

less.

I asked him to describe
the color blue to me.
He couldn't,
so I told him now you know
better how you hurt me.

If I ever
get back
to where I used to be,
I can promise you
I will never go back
to who I was.

ABJECT LONELINESS IS WHEN EITHER A GREAT THING OR ~~terrible~~ **THING HAPPENS TO YOU AND YOU HAVEN'T ANYONE TO SHARE IT WITH.**

All it takes

is one good person

to change your life—

let that person be

you.

She wasn't a wreck.
She was just a fender bender
who crashed into the truth
much more bravely
than she ever swerved
into condoning a lie.

THE TRUTH

DOESN'T BELONG TO ANY OF US.

BUT IT IS ALWAYS OWED

TO THE PERSON YOU LOVE.

We'll watch the stars

burnout the night

'til the morning skies.

There I'll make all

your pain and grief

my own

and wear it in disguise.

I am not searching
for the most beautiful
woman *in the world.*
I am searching
for the most beautiful
woman *in the world to me.*

I've spent
so much of my time
**trying to create
a family**
that I never had,
that I became conditioned
to losing that family
I always wanted.

Your words
don't hurt me,
but your silence does.
And just so you know,
loving you
was far easier
than liking you ever was.

Two people
always find a way

if

they both
want a way.

All your **empty** promises

I've redacted from my memory.

The storybook that was once us

is now just blank pages bound by

nothingness.

DATING:

where you just get
tired of dressing up
and telling your story

again.

Just because you
two clicked
doesn't mean
he or she isn't
still swiping right.
Intuition is soft.
Desire is loud.
Trust the frequency.

SHE WAS BOTH

A WORK OF FICTION
AND NONFICTION.

I TOLD HER I WANTED TO

START WITH HER LIES,

THEN WORK MY WAY

DOWN TO
HER TRUTH.

is a sweater turned inside out
and a belt loop missed
on a pair of pants.
It's forgetting
the order of things
and not giving two fucks.

I am
many things
to many people.
But what matters most
is what I
I am
to myself.

You can fill your days and nights with friends and drink and idle distraction, and they shall occupy your mind and keep the noise of me and the reminder of me at bay for a while. But, in those quiet solitary moments in between, when time and space are your only companions, you will think of me and you will miss of me heavily.

You will miss the way I loved and doted upon you: when how you slept

I bestowed upon you silent kisses all over your tender body and when you were awake, I bestowed upon you your every living wish. You will miss the erotic, hypnotic scent of my skin—the type of scent of mine that will remind you of my strong presence but also of my softest most elegant touch. You will miss the contrast of your pale, slender fingers upon my olive-colored skin. When I heaved with delight, your fingers were in concert with me, and the music we made was conducted by a maestro of our most melodic desire. But mostly, you will miss my eyes: you will miss them like a **ship in stormy weather during the pitch dark of night, where the Earth's jagged rocks mark,** scar, and sink you because the lighthouse that were once my eyes that at one time, too, guided and beamed only for you, have all but been completely snuffed out. When each these things do happen, to which each inevitably will, you will long for me in ways you have only read or heard about.

And in that moment, you will know for a certainty that you love me. And in that same exact moment, you will also know for a certainty that I am long, long gone.

I am turned outside in. I take pills to sleep and pills to wake up. Once up, the first thing that I do is grab for my phone where then, more times than not, I feel that pang of disappointment. Why? No doubt that we all feel that same injury when no one has thought of us. And even if they did, they didn't bother contacting us any more than we felt like being contacted by someone we didn't want to contact us in the first damn place! This is precisely how I feel about this dreadful piece of "Can you hear me fucking, now?!"

It just goes on and on and on. No end in sight. We check and we wait—and we check and we wait—then, bam! That one contact point that tells us we are still alive, that one sound—that one flash—that one beep—I could scream! **We are all prisoners of this need for edification.** I hate it. You know, the type of thing where if you lose it, well, **you lose it!** Can you feel me now?

WHAT IS
THIS LIFE

BUT A WHISPER UPON A SCREAM,

WHERE **LOVE** ISN'T

SOMETHING THAT WE FIND

BUT, RATHER,

SOMETHING THAT

WE DO.

Don't you succumb

to this world and its pretty temptations.

Stay true to who you are

and never be incongruent

to your belief or spirit.

Believe only this;

the right one
will come along
when you
come along.

When she arched her back and stretched like a cat, I knew what was on her mind. Desire clawed out from her pores, and a soft, sensual moan smoldered forth from her loins. She ached and softly purred in ways only she could when the man she was with made her feel most safe and gave her the elevated place beside him where she belonged. she surrendered the most tender parts of herself to him and held herself accountable. To blame her **LUST** on another, she knew, was foolish and gave her false shelter. It slowly, but surely, weakened her resolve in all the other aspects of her life. Armed thus, she was determined not to be taken advantage of or to take advantage of someone else. Rather, she promised herself when she did give her womanhood to a man, it would only be on the condition of exclusivity **between them.** She knew that this union was no guarantee of a long-term partnership, but her conscience was more at ease, and she was better able to pursue freely the things she thought worthy of herself. She never chastised herself again after this self-revelation as she made it a point to be most conscientious; not just when it came to lust, but also when it came to love. She did this because she knew the line between them can sometimes become blurred, and blinded by **it was the last thing she ever wanted to be.**

Do you not see me any longer? I
walk the same hallways as you, and I wonder,
when you do, what colors you see there upon them?
I see pale, lifeless shades, but I don't recall them
ever being that way before. I went into the bedroom,
the one we never use. I see baby-blue painted on
the walls, and I ask myself why we never changed
the color? The small person that once lived there is
gone, and baby blue is not his color any longer. I
believe he outgrew it long ago, but it appears neither
of us did. It's sad in its way, but *I am smart
enough to realize very few things
I can expect to stay the same,
especially people.*

It's quiet here, now. I love it, and at the same time I hate it. The only noise I do hear from time to time is you moving upstairs, the way you try and quietly slide your feet across the wooden floors as to make the least amount of noise possible. It is so loud to me in those moments, like a herd of rumbling buffalo that tear into my eardrums. **I know it is not the sound you make that bothers me but, rather, it is the person who makes the sound that troubles me.** Are these the small, insignificant things that signal to us that our love has run its course? I believe that they are and I ask myself, why did I stay? Do you not see me any longer? I walk the same hallways as you, and I wonder when you do, what colors do you see there upon them? I see pale, lifeless shades, but I don't recall them ever being that way before. I walk upstairs to see you, and you turn around to look back at me but you don't look at me with your heart anymore, just your eyes. I know this is how I must look to you because love, or the lack of love, is always a reflection of whom we are with. The furniture in our bedroom is just that: furniture. The bed, especially, used to be a place where our love was strongest and made manifest, where each our hopes and dreams took seed, gave birth, then took flight. I don't hate you. I hate myself, though, for not having the courage to break my own heart. Sounds foolish to say and to hear but when you really think about it, there is truth in my words. You begin to walk past me and toward the stairs. Your shoulder brushes up against mine and as it does, I feel the slightest bit of energy pass between us. **Are these the small, insignificant things that signal to us that our love has not run its course?** I believe that they are and I ask myself why didn't I stay?

My feelings
don't frighten me.
They remind me that
I am alive.

I want to be
consumed
and thus consume.

I catch myself sometimes—near the keyboard, mouse in hand, my thoughts twisted and contorted in their vicious way where the pen (so to speak) is, indeed, mightier than the sword. What pound of flesh do or did I take, do or did you take? Do we so easily and without remorse carve up one another like prime rib on a skewer just to be served up warmly for the benefit of so many purveyors of our contemptuous words? Does this validate us? I wonder, and that I wonder and in wondering, I wonder what explanation could there be?

We each stop and look at the car wreck. We know this about ourselves: we will look. I look. We can turn away from neither death nor injury—we are too much fascinated by the suffering of others because we know full well our own. This instinct doesn't make us not human. Rather, I believe it is the very thing that makes us human! Evolution of our species, the necessity of "flight or fight" when judging potential threats to us that is the predicator built into the very fiber of our DNA. We consider ourselves a civilized collective, and if we truly and reasonably are, **where do we draw the line with our baseless criticisms of others?** What imaginary line in the sand must be crossed for us to become cognizant that, ultimately, our wayward words do more damage to ourselves than they do to others? Next time you use your words—next time I use mine—oh that we should give pause. **Think. Consider.** *Who do I want to hurt today? Or, who would I rather make feel good today?*

Now: Free yourself from yourself.

Her heart had been cheated. Her teeth had been stained. Her lips had been sealed. Her mind had been deadened. Her hands had been emptied. Her eyes had been closed. Her hair had been damaged. Her gait had been abbreviated. Her emotions had been edited. Her posture had been realigned.

Oh yes, through the years she is much different now but who among us is not? She could remember very little of her past, and she didn't particularly want or care to reflect upon those vague, painful memories anyhow. **Today, instead, she is more certain and more contented with her future.** She is not a seer, not a jinn, not a prophetess, or any such an arcane being. She is a just a woman possessed with the gift of intuition just like each of her other worldly sisters.

When she uses her formidable power, she is undaunted and fearless, and she easily unmasks those that would conceal themselves from her as she is able to discern their truths just as readily as does she uncover their lies. But this knowledge does not please her or make her feel ascendant or impervious to the discovery—oh no, it pulls at her and weighs her down, but burdened thus, she is no less strong. She finds a sort of peace within this strength because she sees far beyond herself, which grants her grace which, in turn, gives her a quiet, soft humility. She may indeed be broken, but she is far from alone, and in this fellowship, she is most intact.

Who will have your heart again?

No one will.

Why won't anyone ever have it?

Because it's gone.

Where did it go?

It left with another.

Do you think you can get it back?

Do we ever get time back?

No, I suppose not, but we both agreed that I was to ask the questions and you were to just answer them.

That wasn't a question.

But I had to let you know that we had gotten off track in our interview.

That wasn't a question, either.

Fair enough.

Ah, you did it again!

Oh, I believe I see where this headed, and I will make certain I am more careful with you in the future by constructing each of my statements as a question: what do you think about that?

I think you are catching on.

Good, may we start over?

We can try to.

I would like it very much if you would just indulge me a moment longer: will you?

Yes, I will do my best.

How do you feel without a heart?

Alone, afraid, anxious, lifeless, dark, ugly, numb, fat, thin, starved, bloated, nauseous, searching, floating, hopelessness, and a sense of never-ending.

If love were to come and try to mend your heart again, would you even recognize it for what it is?

I doubt it.

Why not?

I think because when you've been in the dark for so long it becomes your only trusted, faithful companion. You begin to build a certain bond, an unbreakable partnership that you come to depend upon entirely, and there is a type of comfort in this.

So, in short, you are saying that you learn to adapt to your forlorn situation and this becomes your new reality?

Yes, something like this.

Then, with all hope and promise gone and no heart to give, what do you live for?

I don't really know the answer to that question.

Would you like for me to take you away from here?

Yes.

Do you care where we go?

No.

Can you close your eyes?

Yes.

Can you stop to breathe while your eyes are closed?

For a minute, perhaps.

With your eyes closed and while holding your breath, do you hear something?

I do.

What do you hear?

A beating.

Does it sound like a heart?

Yes.

Can you tell me whose heart it is?

No.

Do you think it is your heart beating?

No, I can't really tell, but I do hear a beating.

Well, it is a heart; it's just not your heart that you hear—it is mine.

Hey, that wasn't a question!

I know, but it is the answer.

Who are you, anyway?

I am the one who will share my heart with you.

Hey, that wasn't a question, either. I know, but it is *the answer*.

May I ask you a few more questions?

Yes.

Do you believe in God?

Yes, I do.

Why do you believe in God?

Because I chose to.

Can you see God?

No, but all around me I see His faithful works: animals, flowers, mountains, rivers, oceans, stars, clouds, the sun, the moon.

Do you think that in believing in something you can't see is called faith?

I do.

Can you see your heart?

No.

Do you think it's inside you beating away?

I do.

Why?

Because I am here speaking with you, and if I didn't have a heart, my blood would never reach my vital organs, and I would be dead.

So, now you choose to believe you have a heart?

Yes, in a manner of speaking but only for myself and not enough to give away to someone else.

Isn't that selfish?

Maybe, but what I have left I am very much in need of.

Do you recall that I gave you my heart?

I did hear you say those words, yes.

Do you know why I gave my heart to you?

No, I don't. Because, like yourself, I have faith in the Lord, and also like you, I choose to believe.

You made a mistake again: that was a statement and not a question.

I know, but it is *the answer*.

A woman
will not believe you
if you tell her
you are different;
she will only believe you
if you show her.

There is just something about you. Why is it do I think I could love you so much? I think it might in the way you like me: the way you look at me, the way sometimes, ironically, you can't look at me at all because it might reveal too much of your heart to me—but, avoiding eye contact with me tells me all I need to know. If you are scared to love, believe me, I am too. It's not my fear of suffering—oh no—it's the fear I may disappoint you and in so doing, disappoint myself. I haven't much to give because I feel all dried up. I've lost so many things dear to me, and those losses have taken a heavy toll. When things we lose or die that we cherish, they take a bit of you with them. When pieces of yourself are gone, this changes your composition. We are not more for our suffering but less. Not less better. Not less hopeful. Not less loving. It's just that we have less to share of ourselves, and it simply cannot be helped—it is just the way of things. I love you no less, I just have less to love you with.

We don't own people; we only own ourselves and even then just fragments at best, because sometimes our mind has, well, a mind of its own. Buddha teaches that all attachment to others will always be self-imbued with suffering. He is correct, in my humble estimation. But, what of attachment to ourselves? Can there be parts we can completely release that are the very definition of who we are, either directly or indirectly? Can our subconscious, which is master of so much of our thought, behavior, and action, ever be disassociated from our consciousness so that we may become truly enlightened? And by enlightened, I don't mean solvent in our knowledge or accredited in our wisdom but, rather, *enlightened in such a way that we know full well our own failings and imperfections so that therefore, we must be tolerant of ourselves just as much as we are of others, if not even more so.*

Self-love
is the right to
contradict yourself
at no one else's expense.

I know what love is.

Yes, you do for a certainty because when you love someone or something, itinvariably hurts.

But why must it hurt to know that you love? Well, have you ever loved and it not hurt?

Yes, I believe that I have.

Really? How did it not hurt?

Well, I only felt this immense attraction, and I couldn't keep my hands off him, and we had so many things in common, and everything between us was just easy—we seemed to flow in all things and always in the same direction.

Wouldn't that make it love?

Yes, it would.

But let me ask you another question, a more exacting one.

Yes?

Are you still together with this person?

No, I am not.

Why did you two part ways?

Because I met someone else who I am actually more attracted to, and he makes me laugh until I literally cry.

Interesting. And, do you miss this other person that you once felt love for?

Not at all!

And you feel nothing for him now—no pain, no regret, no anguish?

Not a one!

Have you seen this person out with another woman?

Yes.

And how did that make you feel?

I couldn't have cared less!

Then I put this to you: you were not in love. That was just your idea of love. That was lust, an attraction, a calibrated harmony of two physical beings that confused love with a more base desire, which led you to confuse the emotions. It is common enough, and I don't ridicule you for your mistake. We've all made it-in fact, it is a necessary component to distinguish between lust and love.

I see your point.

Do you?

I think I do.

Okay, let's do a simple thing to test my theory, okay?

Sure.

This new more attractive, funnier person, are you still together?

Yes.

Do you love him?

Yes, very much.

Why?

Because I don't see him as much as I did the other guy and I miss him like crazy!

Why do you not see him as much?

Well, I am embarrassed to admit it, but he is married. Ah, I see.

Does it hurt?

Yes it does, very much.

Why does it hurt?

Because he told me he would never leave his wife, but that he loves me.

Then I put this to you: you were not in love. That was just your idea of love. That was a lust, an attraction, a calibrated harmony of two physical beings that confused love with a more base desire, which led you to confuse the emotions.

Then please help me to define love, Father?!

Listen and I will.

Love is thus: your body will pulsate with an indescribable energy. Your love will be available to you entirely and not even remotely beholden to someone else. All things you see will appear different, better, brighter, softer, less harsh. You will feel stronger and have a greater pity towards the disenfranchised and the poverty-stricken. You will want to just blend in with your love and camouflage yourself from the world on most days. You will be more patient. You will listen more and talk less. You will see the injustices of a world gone awry, and your empathy will be most overwhelming. You will want to mend broken relationships. You will want to renew old ones. And all these things are beautiful and so welcome in your life!

But, be very aware. Each has their cost, for none are meant to last or, at least, last in the way you view and perceive time. I, your Father, blink and a century passes by. You blink and but a second is gone. Life here on this planet is perishable. There is a shelf life, and the products of each our lives have expiration dates, most especially true love. Before you think I am cruel, consider this: even if you truly love a man as I have described above until the end and until you meet death, either of you, there is still going to be pain associated to that passing. The two, both the pain and the love, are intrinsically bound to one another. There is no way to circumvent them, they can never be sundered, and there is no way to not have one without having the other. So, rejoice and understand their union and accept that inevitability. Knowing this will bring you love. Knowing this will bring you peace.

Friends
with benefits?
I don't think so.
How about a
lover
with a
loyalty
program?

All the same, in the end, we are all the same. No color, no creed, no race may differentiate us. The world we inhabit is primarily constructed of pain. The grey architecture is angled and curved and even misshapen, the most visible commonality is of strife and of struggle, where the each of us try so desperately to carve out but a niche of personal happiness and but a particle of hopeful respite. We are all brothers and sisters of gloom, and this bond is made more salient by the way in which each of us claws and scratches and maims one another for a promise that never can be quite fulfilled, a promise heard on the wind or in a dream, where others we know, or don't know, may claim them as their own and in their possession make it appear more real to us than not. In such lasting effect does envy further taint and disillusion us, our suffering soul. Where one thing is not enough so two things are needed more, but then the two is gained and even that not enough, so four is needed that much more—and on and on and on and so on it goes. We are not happy and are we hardly even close to content and, in the end, we are each so truly the same as again no color, no creed, no race may differentiate us. A circular rock, wrought of pain and gross negligence, is our worldly inheritance, and, brothers and sisters, we are each the beneficiaries so that if we were ever really given a choice, we would much prefer never to have to make claim.

THAT'S RIGHT.

WE NEVER GET EVERYTHING WE WANT,

AND IF WE DID, WHAT BEAUTY COULD BE LEFT

TO THE THINGS AND PERSONS

WE ARE FINALLY BLESSED WITH?

GOD IS INEFFABLE—HIS PLAN IS ETERNAL,

AND NO MORTAL CAN BEAR WITNESS TO IT

BEFORE THE TIME IT HAS ARRIVED TO US

AND COME ACROSS OUR PATH.

THAT IS WHY WE HAVE FAITH,

AND THAT IS WHY WE ENDURE

IN OUR BELIEF IN HIM

AND IN ALL OF HIS

CREATIONS.

I remain in faith
because my firm belief
in religion is not built on the foundations of men but, rather,
on the Word of God.

***

I have come
to the conclusion
that the more
I give advice
to others,
the more I am
really giving
it to myself.

LIFE

is a

CONSTANT

RECOVERY.

I HAVEN'T THE SLIGHTEST INTEREST

IN BEING HAPPY.

I MUCH PREFER TO LIVE LIFE PASSIONATELY,

WHICH IS INARGUABLY MORE DANGEROUS

BUT INCALCULABLY MORE REWARDING,

BECAUSE I MEASURE MY EFFECT

UPON OTHERS NOT BY WHAT

I FEEL IN MY OWN HEART

BUT, RATHER, BY THE LOOK

I SEE UPON THE FACES OF PEOPLE

THAT I COME INTO DIRECT CONTACT WITH.

And neither her bravery
nor her conviction was
stunted nor altered
by what others might have thought
of her but, rather,
they were each made most inviolate,
for she was a woman
who wore her truth
as she did a crown,
and her bearing resembled a
scepter for majestically
and unashamedly
did she carry herself.

We are so busy lately
with erasing history
that I think we
have forgotten
how important
it is to make it.

People give you
the answer
IN FOUR WAYS:
what they say,
what they do,
what they don't say,
and what they don't do.

I remember a time when we hated calculus instead of our neighbor. I remember getting a call on the house phone from a girlfriend that made me more joyous than a text from one by mobile phone today remember throwing the football on concrete streets with friends instead of throwing rocks at our police I remember that if the gym coach gave you a swat, you damn well had it coming, and you didn't get the right to sue either him or the school. I remember saying a pledge each morning that provided routine, endowed calm reassurance, and gave me pause for a moment to think of nothing else but what I said although I didn't necessarily know what it meant I remember scores were settled by the bike rack with fists, and we chased by foot the girls we liked to show our adolescent interest. We held open doors. We said "yes, ma'am" and "no, sir," and the quickest way to a "time out" wasn't on a basketball court or a football field, but by coming home past the hour expected by our bosses: our parents I remember the simple things back then compared to a world today that is full of complexity and too much choice. We used to be a simple people, and by simple I don't mean ignorant or easily impressed. We were satisfied in ways we can't be today because we are constantly bombarded with faster and newer information and transfixed by artificially enhanced images that make us value less what we have next to us already and, worse, makes us question our own self-worth.

I remember those days
And those days remember me.

I'd reckon that
most of our hurt in our lives
comes through
relationships,
so it stands to reason that
healing comes from the very same source.
Looking back, I see there is most likely a lot
we would have done differently
in response to our pain,
that it is very usually laced
with much regret
and what-was-I-thinking moments
of terrible realization.
But what I find more astounding is that
in every love we've ever had,
there was a moment in each that the world
stopped on its axis, then begin to spin unnaturally
again the other way, and for the briefest of moments
we felt how God must always feel
because the rarest gift He gives us
is a reason to love yet again.
Have faith.
Believe in prayer.

I AM FROZEN.

**TOO AFRAID TO MOVE FORWARD AND TOO
ALONE TO LOOK BACK.
SO I SIT SOLID IN PLACE,
WAITING FOR SOMETHING OR SOMEONE
TO THAW ME OUT.
I AM THE FEELING YOU GET
WHEN YOU WATCH YOUR DOG SLOWLY DYING
AND JUST LIKE THE PAINFUL CHOICE YOU HAVE TO
MAKE TO SEND HIM BEYOND HIS SUFFERING.
I AM THE FEELING YOU GET LIKE THAT CHILD
WE ALL KNOW WHO IS FORCED TO IDLE
IN THE "PURGATORY OF NO CHOICE" LIVING
WITH ONLY ONE PARENT BECAUSE
DIVORCE BECAME A BETTER,
MORE SUITABLE SOLUTION FOR THE PARENTS.
I AM THE FEELING YOU GET
WHEN THE PHONE RINGS AT AN HOUR
THAT ONLY BRINGS TERRIBLE NEWS.
I AM THE FEELING YOU GET
WHEN YOU HAVE NO MORE FEELING TO GIVE.
I AM FEELING YOU GET WHEN
WHAT YOU HAD IS NOW ALL GONE.**

I AM THE FEELING.
I AM THE GET.
I AM THE FROZEN.

I am a cloud...

*I am floating with not enough sun
to dissipate me nor enough rain to sustain me.
So I float ... never really touching down
but always hovering over things just beyond my reach ...
I sometimes cast a shadow
and I sometimes extend my shade ...
I am a cloud ...
you can see me and I can see you ...
When you see me I can take the form
of anything you can imagine in your mind:
a bird, a dragon, an angel, a God ...
But, when I look down upon you,
I see myself just like you but just out of touch
and just beyond my grasp ...*

**Distance and,therefore, time separates us
just as assuredly as our yearning does cojoin us,
and, just as you long to be up here,
I long to be down there ...
I am a cloud.**

Did I dream this?

A mother's son was on the ground drowning in a pool of his own blood when from nowhere came up a man to help by trying to staunch the bleeding and give him CPR. As the man lay there looking up at his rescuer, the dying man spoke these words with tears and a soft, bright glow in his eyes

> *"I have a mother whose husband she left because he beat her and told her lies. I hope she finds a man just like you that will rescue her and provide for her."*

He continued but with less energy as the blood flowed out of him even more freely.

> *"I also have two younger sisters who never complain even though they barely have nice clothes to wear to school or more than one pair of shoes each between them. I hope my little sisters meet a man like you to marry when they get older because I am certain you will always do what you can to take care of their needs."*

As the man's breathing grew more labored and his face turned even paler, he forced out these last words to the kind stranger:

> *"I never had a father who taught me anything, mostly because he was not around much. When I was smaller I wished and prayed every night to myself to have a man and father like you in my life."*

With these final words his life left him, and the mysterious stranger who had gently cradled his head the entire time, let out a deep sigh and, finally, he quietly spoke these words into the dead man's ear: "

> *My son I have always been by your mother's side, your sisters' side, and by your side, for I am God almighty, and each of you live eternally through my Word. In this world you shall surely perish, but you shall live everlasting up above in My name and in My glory."*

Did you miss me while you were looking for yourself?

Did you think you'd ever wake up alone from the dream we had built? Did you think our song would ever make you cry because it sound- ed different without me? Did you think your courage would forsake you when you tried to go inside the places we used to visit together? Did you ever imagine a road, a sign, or building could be so deserted when you alone travelled upon it, passed it, or near it? Did you know the wind would blow differently, that the sun would shine less warm, and that the stars would not be as bright? Did your food not taste as good, did the wine make you not remember to for- get, and did the dessert not taste as sweet? Did you realize what you had, had you as much as you had yourself? Did you imagine that my smell could not be conjured up at your whim? Did you know my fingers would leave prints own your soul? Did you know my voice could be heard in any tongue? Did you know we now pray for different things? Did you know our God was always the same? Did you know our last kiss, did you know our last embrace, and did you know those were the last of each of them?

Would you have stopped time? Would time
have stopped you? There is no such thing
as truly living in the present because every-
thing we see still takes a millisecond for our
brain to register and, in that slight lag, time
becomes but a memory. So take heart, lost
lovewatchtower we each live life but a fraction
in the past.

THERE ARE

TWO SIDES

TO EVERYONE.
THEREFORE, IT IS
IMPERATIVE TO BE WITH A PERSON
THAT BRINGS OUT THE
BEST AND NOT THE WORST OF YOU.

THAT IS THE REAL QUESTION
WE MUST EACH ASK OURSELVES:
DO WE STAY WITH OUR PARTNER BECAUSE IT
FAMILIAR EVEN IN ITS PAIN OR,
DO WE LEAVE BECAUSE WE EACH KNOW
THAT IT FAR BETTER AND HEALTHIER
FOR US TO DO SO?
**THE ANSWER IS NEVER EASY
AND ACTION, EVEN HARDER.**
BUT THESE FALSE BONDS THAT BIND
ARE BUT ILLUSIONS WE TELL OURSELVES
TO BRING COMFORT AND JUSTIFICATION
TO STAYING EVEN WHEN WE ARE FULLY AWARE
THAT THE RELATIONSHIP HAS RUN ITS COURSE.
THE TRUTH IS A HARD THING,
BUT IN ITS HARDNESS WE FIND OURSELVES
TRUNCATED TO THE BAREST OF ELEMENTS
AND DISTILLED TO THE MOST BASIC OF REDUCTIONS—
A FREE FORM ABLE TO RECAPTURE WHAT WE ONCE WERE
AND WHAT WE STILL PLAN ON BEING
**WHEN WE CHOOSE
SIMPLY TO LET GO.**

It is often said
that God does not give us more than we can handle.
I have often thought and
carefully considered
this universal Christian saying
and belief and, of late,

I have come to a very different conclusion:
I believe
God does indeed give us more than we can handle
so that we will
know Him,
need Him,
speak to Him,
and rely on Him
even more.

"I love you."

Have there ever been more powerful words?
These words have launched ships.
These words have captured our imagination.
These words have enslaved our soul.
These words have helped us fend off
and to better battle our own fears.
These words have surrendered our
more base human emotions.
These words have indentured our servitude
These words have lifted us above and beyond
the ramparts of our own limitations.
And these words have
caused many a war to see us
the victor upon the battlefield,
where death or loss may eventually precede
and indeed consume us,
but the memory itself sustains life
even when the heart can beat no more.

Heaven

is where you are completely reunited
with all the things you've ever lost:
Your keys. Your dog.
Those earrings. Your mind.
Your soul. That sibling.
Your drive. That money.
That friend. Your heart.
Your time. That Summer.
Your self. Your purse.

That smell. Your wallet.
Your dad. Your belief.
Those pants. Your voice.
That touch. Your way.

That love.

Your mom. Those memories. Your magic. That joy.
Your reason. That race. Your touch. Your grandparent.
That fight. That game. Those glasses. That hope …
And that which we once were
or might have ever hoped to have been.

I want to live inside
the sprawl of your dark, lovely hair.
I want to grow as it grows,
down past your shoulders
just upon such unequivocal
and distinct feminine beauty,
where none but God
can gift such inalienable a blessing.
Sweep them, the ebony strands back now,
just away from your steely eyes,
from those remarkably perfect teeth.
I see a tear quietly smear,
then lightly stream down.
Whose, I ask?
"Yours",
softly she says.

Sometimes you
suddenly awake
in the
middle of the night and
you find yourself

getting
older.

It is then you realize
that all you have left is
a few guitars,
a bag of clothes,
and some

hard
memories

that are
best thought about
only during the day.

I have

W A I T E D

a **L O N G** time for SOMEONE

to make me
a priority
in their life

LIKE I HAVE MADE

a priority
of them

IN MY OWN LIFE,

only to be disappointed to discover that what

they **want** the most

IS NOT IN PRECISE ALIGNMENT

with what

they **need** most.

So, if ever you are fortunate enough
to happen upon someone where
BOTH THEIR WANT AND THEIR NEED
should precisely align,

you will know it

because not only will they
CONSISTENTLY **TELL** YOU,
but they will
CONSISTENTLY **SHOW** YOU.

214

AND JUST LIKE SHE WAS GONE.

LIKE A LIT CIGAR WHOSE ASHES HAD BEEN TAPPED,
SHE FELL INTO THE OCEAN
WHERE HER FIRE HAD BEEN SNUFFED OUT,
AND WITH IT, TOO, HERVAGUE MEMORY
WAS BURIED FROM ME,
LIKE SOME PADDED TREASURE CHEST
THAT HAD SUNK TO THE BOTTOM OF
THE SAME SEA, WHOSE CONTENTS
SEEMED MUCH MORE VALUABLE
SIMPLY BECAUSE I DIDN'T KNOW
WHAT SECRETS SHE POSSESSED,
FOR SHE KEPT THEM HIDDEN FROM ME,
BUT NOT OUT OF SIMPLE GREED,
BUT OUT OF A DARKER FEAR SHE HELD
IN CHECK CLOSELY TO HER OWN HEART,
MAINTAINED SAFELY THERE,
AND LOCKED AWAY DEEP, DEEP INSIDE.

LOVE
IS THE
HARDEST
THING
YOU'LL
EVER
DO.

"I don't fit
into this world."

"Do you not?"

"No, I don't believe so."

"Well, I love you
and because I do, I can
help you
better fit."

I have a lot of respect
and admiration for women.
But, if you continue
to promote the

WRONG
IMAGE,
you will continue
to attract the
WRONG
GUY.

THE GREATEST

tragedy

IS A CHILD MADE TO BELIEVE

THAT SHOWING LOVE

TOWARD ONE PARENT

IS AN ACT OF

betrayal

TO THE OTHER.

Sin(i)sister

(Working Title)
Excerpts of a work of fiction to come.

Who is Elizabeth and what is she about?

Meet Elizabeth Moore, a twenty-nine year old prostitute in New York City who yearns for escape to a better life. From her wrecked childhood, to some of the city's seediest streets and into the arms and confines of some of New York's most beautiful and powerful people, she begins her ascent through society. Beginning with her step-father's abusiveness to her dead mother's uncanny advice, she is set upon a course where she will meet a host of unlovable, corrupt, unforgettable characters as her social rise is overseen by assorted preening socialites, wayward husbands, drunken detectives and, untrustworthy whores of all kinds, and these are the good people: the Devil has yet to call upon her. But he will...

Sin(i)sister

I've become so numb to the pain. Every single day . . . each day like the one before it and each day thereafter, the exact same ... a kaleidoscope of sameness reflected upon every single thing I see. Each day is turned not to vivid color but to a lifeless palette of black and white set upon a canvas of incessantly moving parts, populated by faceless people who go about their day returning to homes or streets diseased with immoral deed and carnal thought. Waxed stick figures we've become: stretched to our limits, bent to the will of people even more corrupt than ourselves, emaciated from enlightened thought, and starved for purpose in a world that glorifies riches and beauty beyond graceful humility and the composition of one's character. A vigilante is needed to cleanse and debunk this myth we call wealth and happiness, a sole purveyor of death that would rather take risks and assume adventures than stagnant in a cesspool of self- delusion.

She would be creature of the night who doesn't stalk its prey, but, rather lures it in with the promise of sex and of sweet release. I would own the streets this night, and if there is a God, let him show his face soon because if he doesn't, then the Devil may very well write a book of his own.

That is why you always text me so late at night with either whiskey or wine on your mind and just sex on your breath. With that we would both laugh uncontrollably, and she would not be able to help herself and snort out loud, which would only cause us to laugh longer and still more until neither of us could catch our breath! When we did finally stop, we would both just lie there on our backs and look up at the ceiling. Where I saw only darkness and infinity, I imagined she saw light and some kind of absolutism.

She had a life to return to, a husband, and one son. I had no one, and my family consisted of long- lost memories and faded, parched dreams. Where she had an oasis, I had but a mirage.

This was when she was the sweetest and kindest and she would try and comfort me, and I was grateful because I knew she meant every word of it. "Liz, we are both lonely. We both long for contented hearts. But don't rush to judgement and think I am better off than you. Just ask yourself this, and be honest with yourself— is it better to be lonely by yourself or, is it better to be lonely with someone you're stuck with but don't love?" I didn't answer, and she didn't press me for one. She quickly got up from the bed, took out a brush from her purse, and combed her hair. Then she put her expensive clothes and shoes on, straightened up her posture, placed eight $100 bills on one of my two nightstands, and walked out the front door with not so much as a backwards glance.

My Love Life,

Sometimes people come into our lives to change our trajectory. That it is why I don't believe in coincidences and that I only believe in circumstances. I hope you are not being too hard on yourself, and I more sincerely hope you begin again to live life in the present. The past is a very harsh mistress, and she wants nothing more than to have you all to herself. But she is only capable of loving in the worst types of ways because she knows there is another beyond her, and this doesn't sit well, so she desperately clings to you, and if you aren't strong and courageous enough, you'll never be able to break free of her.

Love, Mom

This was the last letter my mother ever wrote to me. I always kept it with me, and I treasured it beyond all things, especially since it somehow magically retained on its singular, yellowed page the lavender smell my mother scented herself with just before she went out with one of her paramours. As I carefully folded it up and placed it back neatly into the drawer of my nightstand, I looked back over my shoulder and glanced tenderly at the long blonde hair that spilled out from the covers next to me. As I gently moved closer to her body, I could better smell the remnants of last night's pleasures: the delicate bouquet of wine we drank intermingled with the softest hint of her intoxicating perfume, but mostly what I took in was the rarest of spices and the most alluring decadence of her womanhood that rearoused me most immediately!

I must have moved too quickly or too strongly toward her because the spell was broken and, in that precise moment, she turned back to look into my eyes and beckoned sleepily. I said to her, "Please, Elizabeth, go back to bed. You know I have to leave soon, and sleeping next to you is where I always rest my best."

With that she turned back around and became very quiet as I could hardly even hear her breathe. I badly needed my own rest, so I moved closer still to her, put my form behind her form, and gently cupped her breasts, and tender sleep found me quickly once again.

Sin(i)sister

He had lied and disappointed me so often that when I watched his tongue move, it flickered in and out of his mouth like that of a snake. So far removed was I from feeling anything for him, my heart felt like a missing limb—a phantom limb that couldn't pick up and put back together our past, or one that could construct a future where all hope and promise had been severed because this man could not be to true to any one woman. But that wasn't the most painful part for me—oh no! It was something different—so far different that the description escaped me more, I think, out of self-preservation than from the lack of some reassuring adjective we each tell ourselves to make our pain seem manageable and even surmountable. I haven't some profound, enlightened answer for you because, as you well know yourself, the heart is never connected to the mind: they are entirely independent of one another because to function together would make too much sense, and, in our world, the two are not made for such congruent union. Therefore, I felt forced to act out the words lest my mind should implode. Or, am I forced to speak out because my own words are but simple therapy to myself? Who is to say? All I know is this and this for a certainty—this night would be his last, and I would let him seduce me, and I would ardently play my part. But, when the show ended and the curtain had closed and it was time for the player's to come out and take their bow, I would be the only one in this final scene.

His timeless beauty held me in ways that only the stars could. He radiated so brightly that the blanket of darkness that long shrouded my body disappeared to a galaxy far from and unfamiliar to my senses. He shone an astral light from his dark, steely eyes that were not just beauty celestial but curiously more alien of neither doubt nor fear. As I imagined our two bodies furiously ascending and descending to planes beyond my experience, I felt an immense gravitational collapse that told me I was his, no matter the distance of time or the space continuum. If he felt the same way about me, it wasn't his words that convinced me, for he never uttered a thing, nor did the faintest sound eject from his lips; instead, he seemed to just revolve around me, and, in his slow spinning, I felt my own Earth slowly rotate around his. The space that should have separated us before was now just a thin layer of ozone that couldn't even begin to contain us because like his close neighbor, the moon, the more he waxed the less I waned.

It was in that moment of wistful fantasy that his class ended, and my professor called out to me and asked me to stay for a moment longer while the rest of the class was dismissed.

"Absolute fidelity is a thing all men and women seek in their partners, but this a fool's wish, for neither he nor she can no more expect this of themselves. This trait is what they can demand of others with the same type of devotion. It is unfair, unjust, and unreasonable because what compels people to be dishonest is embedded firmly and early in our childhood years when we begin to . . ."

As she listened to her professor speak, his words seemed to drift off and become unintelligible to her. She was more occupied with his beauty than his words yet it was his words that made him so beautiful. Shaking her head from side to side, she hoped to sort out the conundrum that circled and bounced dizzyingly around inside her head. To somewhat assuage what might have made her palms sweat and her face blush even more profusely, she decided to completely tune out the rest of the lecture and put her head upon her desk. In that way she hoped she wouldn't continue to stare at him so sheepishly. But like most things that are forbidden and like most things that are self-destructive, her mind continued to pull and tempt her as even her eyes, allied thus to her brain, thought more thoroughly to betray her. Slowly raising her head and damning herself for her weakness, she cast up her grey eyes upon him and conjured up an image that would leave a birthmark upon her mind and a beauty mark upon her soul.

As the last rays of sunlight filtered through the narrow mullioned window, the light seemed to cast a supernatural glow over his purloined shadow. Radiant, he shone in a simple white tee shirt and faded jeans with a brown thick leather belt and a polished, oversized buckle. He was cavalier in ways that men aren't today. He was in his early forties, with dark hair, eyebrows, and a beard that just began to show the early signs of greying. There was steel in his eyes and scorn on his lips, which curled like those of a lion that need not roar out loudly, if at all, because you knew a lion when you saw one. His straight nose and prominent chin indicated a strong will, which belied his gentler manner and his face, dashingly handsome, displayed a brutal, frightening candor that she knew was immune to lies, tricks, or treason.

She owned only one pair of jeans, and she wore them all the time. If you were to walk next to her and take notice of her, you could recognize this by her disheveled hair and worn-out heels that these were still newer, fresher, and more durable in comparison. They fitted her well, and the strong blue shade still seemed to retain its original color. They were heavily stitched with white thread that traveled down her leg like a track of railroad that connected seamlessly down to her full hips and long, slender legs to ankles that were narrow and elegant. And if you continued to look at her long enough, you sensed by her steady, determined gait that she was not so much in a hurry to go somewhere but more in a hurry to speed away from what might be following her. When she did slow down, it was only to stop for a cup of coffee, which steamed with heat and made small white puffs that wispily escaped the cup into the crisp, frigid air each time after she carefully took a sip. It was in these almost motionless moments that the locomotive of her heart came to a halfway stop and seemed to open and empty the passengers that clung desperately to the depot of her innards: "envy" got off first because He was too important to be judged by the others. "Hate" stepped off second because She was restless and didn't like to be in one place for too long. "Narcissism" scampered off third because She was charmed by Her own reflection and needed more light to better see Herself. "Pride" was fourth to exit and only in this spot because He tripped over Himself when He tried overhastily to go first. "Betrayal" came last as He trailed discreetly after all the others so He could see each wayfarer better before He decided whom He could most easily take advantage of and whom He might be least detected by when He decided to partner up. As she started to move again you could adjudge that she moved less quickly. One would have thought that after the emptying of her baggage she would be lighter and less encumbered, but ironically, this was wasn't the case at all. She seemed weary and downtrodden even, as if many more rugged miles lie ahead her.

What earlier appeared like righteous determination toward a destination now seemed to have been derailed and gone unceremoniously off track. It was in that moment I decided to intervene. I waved her down emphatically like a commuter signaling that they were late for the departure and could not, under any circumstance, afford to miss their transport. As I hurriedly approached her, she turned to face me with grey eyes and amber hair. Neither of us said a word as we each instinctively took one another's hand, and the immediate intimacy I felt was far greater than any lovemaking because to hold hands comfortably and serenely is more the measure of love than almost anything between two people. In silence we regarded one another for what seemed an eternity. Then she spoke softly but confidently to me these words, "You think you know me, but you can't because I hardly even know myself. But this is what I do know: If you think you can seduce me, don't, because I am more skilled at that than any man, including you. I am not property, and you'll not mark me as such with either money or comforts. My intuition is my power and beyond measure when I decide to listen to it, and I did listen to it because I am here now speaking to you. If you think to hurt me or lie to me, that is your choice; it's been done before, and, yet, here I still stand. And last, what you put in is almost always what you'll get out." With that she reached up slightly and kissed me on the lips. She smelled and tasted of vanilla and cinnamon. She must have seen in my eyes I loved her already because the air around us grew warmer and the railroad crossing guard to her soul opened up and she let me safely pass through.

I pulled the amber colored treated hair back from my soft grey eyes and then gently smiled into my vanity mirror and carefully plucked off just one side of the false eye lashes that I had worn the night before. I left it this way without touching the other one and thought to myself, *This is how a fallen angel must feel with only one wing left to guide her.* I arose from my cushioned seat and I readjusted my nightgown to cover the fullness of my breasts. It always seemed that they spilled out from me. I was always self- conscious of their large size because men looked upon them before anywhere else. It's not that I didn't recognize that I am beautiful. On the contrary, but my mind always comes back to those words my deceased mother had told me when I was a young girl:

"Remember, my love life, the most dangerous part of any road is always the one with the most curves!" Back then I had no idea what my mother had meant, but now, since she was a woman, she understood clearly the wisdom and subtle warning of her words. Of course, I didn't let this stop me from putting implants in the week following her mother's death—in fact looking back, "I put these in precisely because you didn't want me to and you left me, mother, too young and too fragile. I did it because they made me feel sexy, and I especially did it because I looked damned good in my dresses and because of the way they filled them out! Nothing so simple as to attract a man, Mother, as you had scolded me when I spoke to you of possibly having the procedure—that was too easy, and men are very easily enticed. I responded—I did it for me, Mother, and me alone."

Letting the lingerie fall to the ground at that moment, I reached up to take my hair with both hands and carefully unclip the extensions. Without them my hair fell just above my shoulders and lacked the density and length the extensions had gave me. With one more look into the mirror, it occurred to me that somehow I felt less feminine. Sitting back down I removed my make-up, a slow process and one I always agonized over. I never really knew the right amount to put on and never really knew what colors suited me best. When I wore too much my mother would playfully poke at me and say, "You've got your war paint on thick tonight, my love life; those cowboys don't stand a chance!"

We would both have a good, quick laugh at this and then she would kiss me on the cheek before I walked out the door and into the night. I would always turn back to her before she closed the door and tell her that I loved her, and she would always look at me and say, "One day you will be more like me than you ever could ever have imagined, and you will say the same things to your daughter. You just wait and see; it is the way of things."

Her heart had been creased and turned back at the edge of the page like a bookmark that reminded her of where she was in her story. She preferred the touch, smell, and feel of books and not the online sort because she was tactile, and when she marked her page, it showed visually her progress, and this seemed a small accomplishment no matter how far along she was or was not. She was a bit discolored from her age and a bit tattered from her travels, but what she held within those pages was her wisdom and her truths, and this made her feel beautiful.

She was quick to share the story of her book with others and even quicker to realize that what she shared with others, they had in many ways experienced the same types of things, too: painful things mostly, adorned with tragedy and decorated in silent suffering—for what can come from the terrible treatment of us by a person who should of cared for us can be a gift waiting to be given and unwrapped by the next person down our line; that helps to break the cycle of abuse and neglect. In these moments it was when she thought most of the weight of her circumstances and felt the briefest of self-pity for herself, but this feeling was quickly effaced because she was certain that somebody in the world had it worse off than herself or, at least, that's what her few friends told her.

Oddly enough she thought, too, of Einstein and always wondered out loud if this was what he meant by his theory of relativity? She doubted it in many ways, but it made sense to her in her own mind, which caused her to giggle at the absurdity of the comparison. And then, in a flash, it came to her: all pain is relative and what is not and what can be universally objective is our loneliness! It was at this part in her book she always stopped to read, and it was in this part her crease was always left intact. One day she hoped to give her book away, and she longed for a partner to help her turn the page; she was certain he was out there and even more certain that he was looking for a great book to read.

THE END

No, Really.

Nick Anthony Russo *left a successful career to pursue his passion for writing. Nick now dedicates his time to writing and creating books that will heal hearts and open minds to the power words can have on the soul. In his second book, Absolutely Maybe, Nick has brought even more inspiration and encourage to everyone. Nick didn't intend to write a book but his love for writing created a new career path that is changing lives. He hopes his words will inspire others to follow their dreams. Nick is an avid reader and lover of history. He rescues dogs, and has one rescue himself named, Lil' G.*

Nick still lives with his mother.
Not really.
His inner circle of friends
is so small, it's a dot.

.

No, Really.